THE NEGRO
IN
ANCIENT
HISTORY

BY EDWARD W. BLYDEN

978-1-63923-029-7

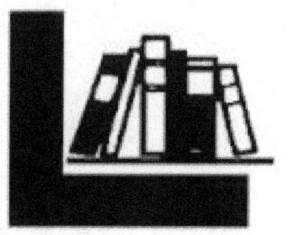

Lushena Books
Publishing
2021

Lushena Books Publishing
Chicago IL
USA

ISBN   978-1-63923-029-7

Copyright 2021

Printed in the United States of America On 100% Acid-Free Paper

The Negro

in

Ancient History

BY EDWARD W. BLYDEN

METHODIST QUARTERLY REVIEW
JANUARY 1869

THE NEGRO

IN

ANCIENT HISTORY.[*]

By EDWARD W. BLYDEN.

PRESUMING that no believer in the Bible will admit that the
negro had his origin at the head waters of the Nile, on the
banks of the Gambia, or in the neighborhood of the Zaire, we
should like to inquire by what chasm is he separated from
other descendants of Noah, who originated the great works of
antiquity, so that with any truth it can be said that "if all
that negroes of all generations have ever done were to be
obliterated from recollection forever the world would lose no
great truth, no profitable art, no exemplary form of life. The
loss of all that is African would offer no memorable deduction
from any thing but the earth's black catalogue of crimes." [†]
In singular contrast with the disparaging statements of the
naval officer, Volney, the great French Oriental traveler and
distinguished linguist, after visiting the wonders of Egypt and
Ethiopia, exclaims, as if in mournful indignation, "How are
we astonished when we reflect that to the race of negroes,
at present our slaves, and the objects of our extreme contempt,
we owe our arts and sciences, and even the very use of

* This is, so far as we know, the first article in any Quarterly written by a hand
claiming a pure Ethiopic lineage.
† Commander Foote, "Africa and the American Flag," p. 207.

speech!" And we do not see how, with the records of the past accessible to us, it is possible to escape from the conclusions of Volney. If it cannot be shown that the negro race was separated by a wide and unapproachable interval from the founders of Babylon and Nineveh, the builders of Babel and the Pyramids, then we claim for them a participation in those ancient works of science and art, and that not merely on the indefinite ground of a common humanity, but on the ground of close and direct relationship.

Let us turn to the tenth chapter of Genesis, and consider the ethnographic allusions therein contained, receiving them in their own grand and catholic spirit. And we the more readily make our appeal to this remarkable portion of Holy Writ because it has "extorted the admiration of modern ethnologists, who continually find in it anticipations of their greatest discoveries." Sir Henry Rawlinson says of this chapter: "The Toldoth Beni Noah (the Hebrew title of the chapter) is undoubtedly *the most authentic* record we possess for the affiliation of those branches of the human race which sprang from the triple stock of the Noachidæ." And again: "We must be cautious in drawing direct ethnological inferences from the linguistic indications of a very early age. It would be far *safer*, at any rate, in these early times, to follow the general scheme of ethnic affiliation which is given in the tenth chapter of Genesis." *

From the second to the fifth verse of this chapter we have the account of the descendants of Japheth and their places of residence, but we are told nothing of their *doings* or their *productions*. From the twenty-first verse to the end of the chapter we have the account of the descendants of Shem and of their "dwelling." Nothing is said of their *works*. But how different the account of the descendants of Cush, the eldest son of Ham, contained from the seventh to the twelfth verse. We read: "And Cush begat Nimrod: he began to be a mighty one in the earth. He was a mighty hunter before the Lord. . . . And the beginning of his kingdom was Babel, and Erech, and Accad, and Calneh, in the land of Shinar. Out of that land he went forth into Asshur, (marginal reading,) and builded Nineveh, and the city Reho-

* Quoted by G. Rawlinson in Notes to "Bampton Lectures," 1859.

both, and Calah, and Resen between Nineveh and Calah: the same is a great city."

We have adopted the marginal reading in our English Bible, which represents Nimrod as having founded Nineveh, in addition to the other great works which he executed. This reading is supported by authorities, both Jewish and·Christian, which cannot be set aside. The author of "Foundations of History," without, perhaps, a due consideration of the original, affirms that Asshur was "one of the sons of Shem!" thus despoiling the descendants of Ham of the glory of having "builded" Nineveh. And to confirm this view he tells us that "Micah speaks of the land of Asshur and the land of Nimrod as two distinct countries." We have searched in vain for the passage in which the Prophet makes such a representation. The verse to which this author directs us (Micah v, 6) is unfortunate for this theory. It is plain from the closing of the verse that the conjunction "*and,*" in the first clause, is not the simple copulative *and* or *also,* but is employed, according to a well known Hebrew usage, in the sense of *even* or *namely,* to introduce the words "land of Nimrod" as an explanatory or qualifying addition in apposition to the preceding "land of Assyria." *

We must take Asshur in Gen. x, 11, not as the subject of the verb "went," but as the name of the place whither—the *terminus ad quem.* So Drs. Smith and Van Dyck, eminent Oriental scholars, understand the passage, and so they have rendered it in their admirable Arabic translation of the Bible, recently adopted by the British and Foreign Bible Society, namely, "Out of that land he (Nimrod) went forth unto Asshur—Assyria—and builded Nineveh." De Sola, Lindenthal, and Raphall, learned Jews, so translate the passage in their "New Translation of the Book of Genesis." † Dr. Kalisch, another Hebrew of the Hebrews, so renders the verse in his "Historical and Critical Commentary on Genesis." ‡ All these authorities, and others we might mention, agree that

---

* See Conant's Gesenius's Hebrew Grammar, (17th edition,) section 155, (a); and for additional examples of this usage see Judges vii, 22; 1 Sam. xvii, 40; Jer. xv, 13, where *even* represents the conjunction *vau* (and) in the original.

† London, 1844.

‡ London, 1858. See Dr. Robinson's view in Gesenius's Hebrew Lexicon, under the word Cush.

to make the passage descriptive of the Shemite Asshur is to do violence to the passage itself and its context. Asshur, moreover, is mentioned in his proper place in verse 22, and without the least indication of an intention of describing him as the founder of a rival empire to Nimrod.* Says Nachmanides, (quoted by De Sola, etc.): "It would be strange if Asshur, a son of Shem, were mentioned among the descendants of Ham, of whom Nimrod was one. It would be equally strange if the deeds of Asshur were spoken of before his birth and descent had been mentioned."

The grammatical objection to our view is satisfactorily disposed of by Kalisch.† On the absence of the ח (*he*) locale he remarks: "The ח locale, after verbs of motion, though frequently, is by no means uniformly, applied. (1 Kings xi, 17; 2 Kings xv, 14; etc.) Gesenius, whose authority no one will dispute, also admits the probability of the view we have taken, without raising any objection of grammatical structure."

But enough on this point. We may reasonably suppose that the building of the *tower of Babel* was also the work, principally, of Cushites. For we read in the tenth verse that Nimrod's kingdom was in the land of Shinar; and in the second verse of the eleventh chapter we are told that the people who undertook the building of the tower, "found a plain in the land of *Shinar*" which they considered suitable for the ambitious structure. And, no doubt, in the "scattering" which resulted, these sons of Ham found their way into Egypt,‡ where their descendants—inheriting the skill of their fathers, and guided by tradition—erected the pyramids in imitation of the celebrated tower. Herodotus says that the tower was six hundred and sixty feet high, or one hundred and seventy feet higher than the great pyramid of Cheops. It consisted of eight square towers, one above another. The winding path is said to have been four miles in length. Strabo calls it a pyramid.

But it may be said, The enterprising people who founded Babylon and Nineveh, settled Egypt, and built the Pyramids,

---

* See Kitto's Biblical Cyclopedia, article, *Ham.* London, 1866.
† Historical and Critical Commentary on Genesis. Heb. and Eng. P. 263.
‡ It is certain that Mizraim, with his descendants, settled Egypt, giving his name to the country, which it still retains. The Arabic name for Egypt is *Misr.* In Psalm cv, 23, Egypt is called "the land of Ham."

though descendants of Ham, were not *black*—were not negroes;
for, granted that the negro race have descended from Ham, yet,
when these great civilizing works were going on the descendants of Ham had not yet reached that portion of Africa, had
not come in contact with those conditions of climate and atmosphere which have produced that peculiar development of
humanity known as the Negro.

Well, let us see. It is not to be doubted that from the
earliest ages the black complexion of some of the descendants
of Noah was known. Ham, it would seem, was of a complexion darker than that of his brothers. The root of the
name Ham, in Hebrew חַם, (Hamam,) conveys the idea of *hot*
or *swarthy*. So the Greeks called the descendants of Ham,
from their black complexion, *Ethiopians*, a word signifying
burnt or *black* face. The Hebrews called them Cushites, a
word probably of kindred meaning. Moses is said to have
married a Cushite or Ethiopian woman, that is, a *black*
woman descended from Cush. The query, "Can the Ethiopian change his skin?" seems to be decisive as to a differ-
ence of complexion between the Ethiopian and the Shemite,
and the etymology of the word itself determines that the complexion of the former was black. The idea has been thrown
out that the three principal colors now in the world—white,
brown, and black—were represented in the ark in Japheth,
Shem, and Ham.

But were these enterprising descendants of Ham *woolly-
haired?*—a peculiarity which, in these days, seems to be
considered a characteristic mark of degradation and servility.*   On this point let us consult Herodotus, called "the
father of history." He lived nearly three thousand years ago.
Having traveled extensively in Egypt and the neighboring
countries, he wrote from personal observation. His testimony

---

* While Rev. Elias Schrenk, a German missionary laboring on the Gold Coast,
in giving evidence on the condition of West Africa before a committee of the
House of Commons in May, 1865, was making a statement of the proficiency
of some of the natives in his school in Greek and other branches of literature, he
was interrupted by Mr. Cheetham, a member of the committee, with the inquiry:
" Were those young men of *pure* African blood?" "Yes," replied Mr. Schrenk,
" decidedly; thick lips and black skin." "And woolly hair?" added Mr. Cheetham. "And woolly hair," subjoined Mr. Schrenk. (See "Parliamentary Report
on Western Africa for 1865," p. 145.)

is that of an eye-witness. He tells us that there were two divisions of Ethiopians, who did not differ at all from each other in appearance, except in their language and hair; "for the eastern Ethiopians," he says, "are straight-haired, but those of Libya (or Africa) have hair more curly than that of any other people."* He records also the following passage, which fixes the physical characteristics of the Egyptians and some of their mighty neighbors : †

> The Colchians were evidently Egyptians, and I say this *having myself observed it* before I heard it from others ; and as it was a matter of interest to me, I *inquired* of both people, and the Colchians had more recollection of the Egyptians than the Egyptians had of the Colchians ; yet the Egyptians said that they thought the Colchians had descended from the army of Sesostris ; and I formed my conjecture, *not only because they are black in complexion and woolly-haired,* for this amounts to nothing, because *others are so likewise,* etc., etc.‡

Rawlinson has clearly shown § that these statements of Herodotus have been too strongly confirmed by all recent researches (among the cuneiform inscriptions) in comparative philology to be set aside by the tottering criticism of such superficial inquirers as the Notts and Gliddons, *et id omne genus,* who base their assertions on ingenious conjectures. Pindar and Æschylus corroborate the assertions of Herodotus.

Homer, who lived still earlier than Herodotus, and who had also traveled in Egypt, makes frequent mention of the Ethiopians. He bears the same testimony as Herodotus as to their division into two sections :

> Αἰθίοπας, τοὶ διχθὰ δεδαίαται, ἔσχατοι ἀνδρῶν,
> 'Οἱ μὲν δυσομένου 'Υπερίονος, οἱ δ' ἀνιόντος— ‖

which Pope freely renders :

> "A race divided, whom with sloping rays
> The rising and descending sun surveys."

---

* Herodotus, iii, 94; vii, 70.

† It is not necessary, however, to consider *all* Egyptians as negroes, black in complexion and woolly-haired; this is contradicted by their mummies and portraits. Blumenbach discovered three varieties of physiognomy on the Egyptian paintings and sculptures; but he describes the general or national type as exhibiting a certain approximation to the Negro.

‡ Herodotus, ii, 104.   § Five Great Monarchies, vol. i, chap. 3.

‖ Odyssey, i, 23, 24.

And Homer seems to have entertained the very highest opinion of these Ethiopians. It would appear that he was so struck with the wonderful works of these people, which he saw in Egypt and the surrounding country, that he raises their authors above mortals, and makes them associates of the gods. Jupiter, and sometimes the whole Olympian family with him, is often made to betake himself to Ethiopia to hold converse with and partake of the hospitality of the Ethiopians.*

But it may be asked, Are we to suppose that the Guinea negro, with all his peculiarities, is descended from these people? We answer, Yes. The descendants of Ham, in those early ages, like the European nations of the present day, made extensive migrations and conquests. They occupied a portion of two continents. While the Shemites had but little connection with Africa, the descendants of Ham, on the contrary, beginning their operations in Asia, spread westward and southward, so that as early as the time of Homer they had not only occupied the northern portions of Africa, but had crossed the great desert, penetrated into Soudan, and made their way to the west coast. "As far as we know," says that distinguished Homeric scholar, Mr. Gladstone, "Homer recognized the African coast by placing the Lotophagi upon it, and the *Ethiopians inland from the East all the way to the extreme West.*" †

Some time ago Professor Owen, of the New York Free Academy, well known for his remarkable accuracy in editing the ancient classics, solicited the opinion of Professor Lewis of the New York University, another eminent scholar, as to the localities to which Homer's Ethiopians ought to be assigned. Professor Lewis gave a reply which so pleased Professor Owen that he gives it entire in his notes on the Odyssey, as "the most rational and veritable comment of any he had met with." It is as follows:

I have always, in commenting on the passage to which you refer, explained it to my classes as denoting the black race, (or Ethiopians, as they were called in Homer's time,) living on the eastern and western coast of Africa—the one class inhabiting the country now called Abyssinia, and the other that part of Africa called Guinea or the Slave Coast. The common explanation that

* Iliad, i, 423; xxiii, 206.
† "Homer and the Homeric Age," vol. iii, p. 305.

it refers to two divisions of Upper Egypt separated by the Nile, besides, as I believe, being geographically incorrect, (the Nile really making no such division,) does not seem to be of sufficient importance to warrant the strong expressions of the text. (Odyssey i, 22–24.) If it be said the view I have taken supposes too great a knowledge of geography in Homer, we need only bear in mind that he had undoubtedly visited Tyre, where the existence of the black race on the West of Africa had been known from the earliest times. The Tyrians, in their long voyages, having discovered a race on the West, in almost every respect similar to those better known in the East, would, from their remote distance from each other, and not knowing of any intervening nations in Africa, naturally style them the two extremities of the earth. (Homer's εσχατοι ανδρων.) Homer elsewhere speaks of the Pigmies, who are described by Herodotus and Diodorus Siculus as residing in the interior of Africa, (on a river which I think corresponds to what is now called the Niger.) It seems to me too extravagant language, even for poetry, to represent two nations, separated only by a river, as living, one at the rising, the other at the setting sun, although these terms may sometimes be used for East and West. Besides, if I am not mistaken, no such division is recognized in subsequent geography.*

Professor Lewis says nothing of the *Asiatic* division of the Ethiopians. But since his letter was penned—more than twenty years ago—floods of light have been thrown upon the subject of Oriental antiquities by the labors of M. Botta, Layard, Rawlinson, Hinks, and others. Even Bunsen, not very long ago, declared that "the idea of an '*Asiatic Cush*' was an imagination of interpreters, the child of despair." But in 1858, Sir Henry Rawlinson having obtained a number of Babylonian documents more ancient than any previously discovered, was able to declare authoritatively that the early inhabitants of South Babylonia *were of a cognate race with the primitive colonists both of Arabia and of the African Ethiopia.*† He found their *vocabulary to be undoubtedly Cushite or Ethiopian,* belonging to that stock of tongues which in the sequel were every-where more or less mixed up with the Semitic languages, but of which we have the purest modern specimens in the "Mahra of Southern Arabia," and the "Galla of Abyssinia." He also produced evidence of the widely-spread settlements of the children of Ham *in Asia as*

---

* Owen's Homer's Odyssey, (Fifth Edition,) p. 306.
† Rawlinson's Herodotus. Vol. i, p. 442.

well as Africa, and (what is more especially valuable in our present inquiry) of the truth of the tenth chapter of Genesis as an ethnographical document of the highest importance.*

Now, we should like to ask, If the negroes found at this moment along the West and East coast, and throughout Central Africa, are not descended from the ancient Ethiopians, from whom are they descended? And if they are the children of the Ethiopians, what is the force of the assertions continually repeated, by even professed friends of the negro, that the enterprising and good-looking tribes of the continent, such as Lalofs, Mandingoes, and Foulahs, are mixed with the blood of Caucasians?† With the records of ancient history before us, where is the necessity for supposing such an admixture? May not the intelligence, the activity, the elegant features and limbs of these tribes have been directly transmitted from their ancestors?

The Foulahs have a tradition that they are the descendants of Phut, the son of Ham. Whether this tradition be true or not, it is a singular fact that they have prefixed this name to almost every district of any extent which they have ever occupied. They have Futa-Torro, near Senegal; Futa-Bondu and Futa-Iallon to the north-east of Sierra Leone.‡

Lenormant was of the opinion that Phut peopled Libya.

We gather from the ancient writers already quoted that the Ethiopians were celebrated for their beauty. Herodotus speaks of them as "men of large stature, *very handsome* and long-lived." And he uses these epithets in connection with the Ethiopians of *West Africa,* as the context shows. The whole passage is as follows:

Where the meridian declines toward the setting sun (that is, southwest from Greece) the Ethiopian territory reaches, being the extreme part of the habitable world. It produces much gold, huge elephants, wild trees of all kinds, *ebony,* and men of large stature, *very handsome,* and long-lived.§

Homer frequently tells us of the "handsome Ethiopians," although he and Herodotus do not employ the same Greek word. In Herodotus the word that describes the Ethiopians

---

* See Article *Ham,* in Kitto's Cyclopedia.   Last Edition.
† Bowen's "Central Africa," chap. xxiii.   ‡ Wilson's Western Africa, p. 79.
§ Herodotus, iii, 114.

is καλος—a word denoting both beauty of outward form and moral beauty or virtue.* The epithet (αμυμων) employed by Homer to describe the same people is by some commentators rendered "blameless," but by the generality "handsome." Anthon says: "It is an epithet given to all men and women distinguished by rank, exploits, or beauty."† Mr. Hayman, one of the latest and most industrious editors of Homer, has in one of his notes the following explanation: "Αμυμων was at first an epithet of distinctive excellence, but had become a purely conventional style, as applied to a class, like our ' honorable and gallant gentleman.'"‡ Most scholars, however, agree with Mr. Paley, another recent Homeric commentator, that the original signification of the word was "handsome," and that it nearly represented the καλος καγαθος of the Greeks; § so that the words which Homer puts into the mouth of Thetis when addressing her disconsolate son (Iliad, i, 423) would be, "Yesterday Jupiter went to Oceanus, to the *handsome* Ethiopians, to a banquet, and with him went all the gods." It is remarkable that the Chaldee, according to Bush, has the following translation of Numbers xii, 1: "And Miriam and Aaron spake against Moses because of the beautiful woman whom he had married; for he had married a beautiful woman." ‖ Compare with this Solomon's declaration, "I am *black* but *comely*," or, more exactly, "I am black *and* comely." We see the wise man in his spiritual epithalamium selecting a black woman as a proper representative of the Church and of the highest purity. The word שׁחוֹרָה, translated in our version *black*, is a correct rendering. So Luther, *schwarz.* It cannot mean *brown*, as rendered by Ostervald (*brune*) and Diodati (*bruna*.) In Lev. xiii, 31, 37, it is applied to hair. The verb from which the adjective comes is used (Job xxx, 30) of the countenance blackened by disease. In Solomon's Song v, 11, it is applied to the plumage of a raven.¶ In the days of Solomon, therefore, black, as a physical attribute, was *comely.*

* Liddell & Scott.　　　　　† Anthon's Homer, p. 491.
‡ Hayman's Odyssey, i, 29.　§ Paley's Iliad, p. 215. Note.　‖ Bush, *in loco.*.
¶ A correspondent of the New York Tribune, residing in Syria, describing the appearance of a negro whom he met there in 1866, says: "He was as *black* as a Mount Lebanon raven." (N. Y. Tribune, October 16, 1866.) Had he been writing in Hebrew he would have employed the descriptive word שׁחוֹר.

But when, in the course of ages, the Ethiopians had wandered into the central and southern regions of Africa, encountering a change of climate and altered character of food and modes of living, they fell into intellectual and physical degradation. This degradation did not consist, however, in a change of color, as some suppose, for they were black, as we have seen, before they left their original seat. Nor did it consist in the stiffening and shortening of the hair; for Herodotus tells us that the Ethiopians in Asia were *straight-haired*, while their relatives in Africa, from the same stock and in no lower stage of progress, were *woolly haired*. The hair, then, is not a fundamental characteristic, nor a mark of degradation. Some suppose that the hair of the negro is affected by some peculiarity in the African climate and atmosphere—perhaps the influence of the Sahara entering as an important element. We do not profess to know the *fons et origo*, nor have we seen any satisfactory cause for it assigned. We have no consciousness of any inconvenience from it, except that in foreign countries, as a jovial fellow-passenger on an English steamer once reminded us, "it is *unpopular.*"

"Vuolsi così colà, dove si puote
Ciò che si vuole: e più non dimandare."*

Nor should it be thought strange that the Ethiopians who penetrated into the heart of the African continent should have degenerated, when we consider their distance and isolation from the quickening influence of the arts and sciences in the East; their belief, brought with them, in the most abominable idolatry, " changing the glory of the incorruptible God into an image made like unto corruptible man, and to *birds*, and *four-footed beasts*, and *creeping things*," Rom. i, 23; the ease with which, in the prolific regions to which they had come, they could secure the means of subsistence; and the constant and enervating heat of the climate, indisposing to continuous exertion. Students in natural history tell us that animals of the same species and family, if dispersed and domesticated, show striking modifications of the original type, in their color, hair, integument, structure of limbs, and even in their instincts, habits, and powers. Similar changes are witnessed

* Dante.

among mankind. An intelligent writer in No. 48 of the "Dublin University Magazine" says:

There are certain districts in Leitrim, Sligo, and Mayo chiefly inhabited by the descendants of the native Irish, driven by the British from Armagh and the South of Down about two centuries ago. These people, whose ancestors were well-grown, able-bodied, and comely, are now reduced to an average stature of five feet two inches, are pot-bellied, bow-legged, and abortively featured; and they are especially remarkable for open projecting mouths, and prominent teeth, and exposed gums, their advancing cheekbones and depressed noses bearing barbarism in their very front. In other words, within so short a period, they seem to have acquired a prognathous type of skull, like the Australian savages.

But these retrogressive changes are taking place in other countries besides Ireland. Acute observers tell us that in England, the abode of the highest civilization of modern times, "a process of de-civilization, a relapse toward barbarism, is seen in the debased and degraded classes, with a coincident deterioration of physical type." Mr. Henry Mayhew, in his "London Labor and London Poor," has remarked that

Among them, according as they partake more or less of the pure vagabond nature, doing nothing whatever for their living, but moving from place to place, preying on the earnings of the more industrious portion of the community, so will the attributes of the nomadic races be found more or less marked in them; and they are all more or less distinguished by their high cheek-bones and protruding jaws; thus showing that kind of mixture of the pyramidal with the prognathous type which is to be seen among the most degraded of the Malayo-Polynesian races.

In contrast with this retrogressive process, it may be observed that in proportion as the degraded races are intellectually and morally elevated, their physical appearance improves. Mr. C. S. Roundell, secretary to the late Royal Commission in Jamaica, tells us that

The Maroons who fell under my (his) own observation in Jamaica, exhibited a marked superiority in respect of comportment, mental capacity, and physical type—a superiority to be referred to the saving effects of long-enjoyed freedom. The Maroons are descendants of runaway Spanish slaves, who at the time of the British conquest established themselves in the mountain fastnesses.*

* "England and her Subject Races, with special reference to Jamaica." By Charles Saville Roundell, M. A.

In visiting the native towns interior to Liberia, we have seen striking illustrations of these principles. Among the inhabitants of those towns we could invariably distinguish the free man from the slave. There was about the former a dignity of appearance, an openness of countenance, an independence of air, a firmness of step, which indicated the absence of oppression; while in the latter there was a depression of countenance, a general deformity of appearance, an awkwardness of gait, which seemed to say, "That man is a slave."

Now, with these well-known principles before us, why should it be considered strange that, with their fall into barbarism, the "handsome" Ethiopians of Homer and Herodotus should have deteriorated in physical type—and that this degradation of type should continue reproducing itself in the wilds of Africa and in the Western Hemisphere, where they have been subjected to slavery and various other forms of debasing proscription?

> Ἥμισυ γάρ τ' ἀρετῆς ἀποαίνυται εὐρύοπα Ζεὺς
> Ἀνέρος, εὐτ' ἄν μιν κατὰ δούλιον ἦμαρ ἕλησιν.*

The Negro is often taunted by superficial investigators with proofs, as is alleged, taken from the monuments of Egypt, of the servitude of Negroes in very remote ages. But is there any thing singular in the fact that in very early times Negroes were held in bondage? Was it not the practice among all the early nations to enslave each other? Why should it be pointed to as an exceptional thing that Ethiopians were represented as slaves? It was very natural that the more powerful Ethiopians should seize upon the weaker, as is done to this day in certain portions of Africa, and reduce them to slavery. And were it not for the abounding light of Christianity now enjoyed in Europe the same thing would be done at this moment in Rome, Paris, and London. For the sites of those cities in ancient times witnessed all the horrors of a cruel and mercenary slave-trade, not in Negroes, but Caucasian selling Caucasian.†

---

* Odyssey, xvii, 322, 323.

† Cicero in one of his letters, speaking of the success of an expedition against Britain, says the only plunder to be found consisted "Ex emancipiis; ex quibus nullos puto te literis aut musicis eruditos expectare;" thus proving, in the same sentence, the existence of the slave-trade, and intimating that it was impos-

But were there no Caucasian slaves in Egypt? If it be true that no such slaves are represented on the monumental remains, are we, therefore, to infer that they did not exist in that country? Are we to disbelieve that the Jews were in the most rigorous bondage in that land for four hundred years:

Not every thing which is not represented on the monuments was therefore necessarily unknown to the Egyptians. The monuments are neither intended to furnish, nor can they furnish, a complete delineation of all the branches of public and private life, of all the products and phenomena of the whole animal, vegetable, and mineral creation of the country. They cannot be viewed as a complete cyclopædia of Egyptian customs and civilization. Thus we find no representation of fowls and pigeons, although the country abounded in them; of the wild ass and wild boar, although frequently met with in Egypt; none of the process relating to the casting of statues and other objects in bronze, although many similar subjects connected with the arts are represented; none of the marriage ceremony, and of numerous other subjects.[*]

But we are told that the Negroes of Central and West Africa have proved themselves essentially inferior from the fact, that in the long period of three thousand years they have shown no signs of progress. In their country, it is alleged, are to be found no indications of architectural taste or skill, or of any susceptibility of æsthetic or artistic improvement; that they have no monuments of past exploits; no paintings or sculptures; and that, therefore, the foreign or American slave-trade was an indispensable agency in the civilization of Africa; that nothing could have been done for the Negro while he remained in his own land bound to the practices of ages; that he needed the sudden and violent severance from home to deliver him from the quiescent degradation and stagnant barbarism of his ancestors; that otherwise the civilization of Europe could never have impressed him.

In reply to all this we remark: 1st, That it remains to be

sible that any Briton should be intelligent enough to be worthy to serve the accomplished Atticus. (Ad. Att., lib. iv, 16.) Henry, in his History of England, gives us also the authority of Strabo for the prevalence of the slave-trade among the Britons, and tells us that slaves were once an established article of export. "Great numbers," says he, "were exported from Britain, and were to be seen exposed for sale, like cattle, in the Roman market."—*Henry*, vol. ii, p. 225. Also, Sir T. Fowell Buxton's "Slave Trade and Remedy"—Introduction.

[*] Dr Kalisch: "Commentary on Exodus," p. 147. London, 1855.

proved, by a fuller explanation of the interior, that there are
no architectural remains, no works of artistic skill ; 2dly, If it
should be demonstrated that nothing of the kind exists, this
would not necessarily prove essential inferiority on the part of
the African.   What did the Jews produce in all the long
period of their history before and after their bondage to the
Egyptians, among whom, it might be supposed, they would
have made some progress in science and art ?   Their forefathers
dwelt in tents before their Egyptian residence, and they dwelt
in tents after their emancipation.   And in all their long
national history they produced no remarkable architectural
monument but the Temple, which was designed and executed
by a man miraculously endowed for the purpose.   A high anti-
quarian authority tells us that "pure Shemites had no art."*
The lack of architectural and artistic skill is no mark of the
absence of the higher elements of character. † 3rdly, With re-
gard to the necessity of the slave trade, we remark, without
attempting to enter into the secret counsels of the Most High,
that without the foreign slave-trade Africa would have been
a great deal more accessible to civilization, and would now,
had peaceful and legitimate intercourse been kept up with her
from the middle of the fifteenth century, be taking her stand
next to Europe in civilization, science, and religion.   When,
four hundred years ago, the Portuguese discovered this coast,
they found the natives living in considerable peace and quiet-
ness, and with a certain degree of prosperity.   Internal feuds,
of course, the tribes sometimes had, but by no means so serious
as they afterward became under the stimulating influence of
the slave-trade.   From all we can gather, the tribes in this

---

* Rev. Stuart Poole, of the British Museum, before the British Association. 1864.
† Rev. Dr. Goulburn; in his reply to Dr. Temple's celebrated Essay on the
"Education of the World," has the following suggestive remark: "We commend
to Dr. Temple's notice the pregnant fact, that in the earliest extant history of mankind it is stated that arts, both ornamental and useful, (and arts are the great
medium of civilization,) took their rise in the family of Cain.   In the line of Seth
we find none of this mental and social development."—*Replies to Essays and
Reviews*, p. 34.   When the various causes now co-operating shall have produced
a higher religious sense among the nations, and a corresponding revolution shall
have taken place in the estimation now put upon material objects, the effort
may be to show, to his disparagement—if we could imagine such an unamiable
undertaking as compatible with the high state of progress then attained—that the
Negro was at the foundation of all material development.

part of Africa lived in a condition not very different from that of the greater portion of Europe in the Middle Ages. There was the same oppression of the weak by the strong; the same resistance by the weak, often taking the form of general rebellion; the same private and hereditary wars; the same strongholds in every prominent position; the same dependence of the people upon the chief who happened to be in power; the same contentedness of the masses with the tyrannical rule. But there was industry and activity, and in every town there were manufactures, and they sent across the continent to Egypt and the Barbary States other articles besides slaves.

The permanence for centuries of the social and political states of the Africans at home must be attributed, first, to the isolation of the people from the progressive portion of mankind; and, secondly, to the blighting influence of the traffic introduced among them by Europeans. Had not the demand arisen in America for African laborers, and had European nations inaugurated regular traffic with the coast, the natives would have shown themselves as impressible for change, as susceptible of improvement, as capable of acquiring knowledge and accumulating wealth, as the natives of Europe. Combination of capital and co-operation of energies would have done for this land what they have done for others. Private enterprise, (which has been entirely destroyed by the nefarious traffic,) encouraged by humane intercourse with foreign lands, would have developed agriculture, manufactures, and commerce; would have cleared, drained, and fertilized the country, and built towns; would have improved the looms, brought in plows, steam-engines, printing presses, machines, and the thousand processes and appliances by which the comfort, progress, and usefulness of mankind are secured. But, alas! *Dis aliter visum.*

> "Freighted with curses was the bark that bore
> The spoilers of the West to Guinea's shore;
> Heavy with groans of anguish blew the gales
> That swelled that fatal bark's returning sails:
> Loud and perpetual o'er the Atlantic's waves,
> For guilty ages, rolled the tide of slaves;
> A tide that knew no fall, no turn, no rest—
> Constant as day and night from East to West,
> Still widening, deepening, swelling in its course
> With boundless ruin and resistless force."—MONTGOMERY.

But although, amid the violent shocks of those changes and disasters to which the natives of this outraged land have been subject, their knowledge of the elegant arts, brought from the East, declined, they never entirely lost the *necessary* arts of life. They still understand the workmanship of iron, and, in some sections of the country, of gold. The loom and the forge are in constant use among them. In remote regions, where they have no intercourse with Europeans, they raise large herds of cattle and innumerable sheep and goats; capture and train horses, build well-laid-out towns, cultivate extensive fields, and manufacture earthenware and woolen and cotton cloths. Commander Foote says: " The Negro arts are respectable, and would have been more so had not disturbance and waste come with the slave-trade."*

And in our own times, on the West Coast of Africa, a native development of literature has been brought to light of genuine home-growth. The Vey people, residing half way between Sierra Leone and Cape Mesurado, have within the last thirty years invented a syllabic alphabet, with which they are now writing their own language, and by which they are maintaining among themselves an extensive epistolary correspondence In 1849 the Church Missionary Society in London, having heard of this invention, authorized their missionary, Rev. S. W. Koelle, to investigate the subject. Mr. Koelle traveled into the interior, and brought away three manuscripts, with translations. The symbols are phonetic, and constitute a syllabarium, not an alphabet; they are nearly two hundred in number. They have been learned so generally that Vey boys in Monrovia frequently receive communications from their friends in the Vey country to which they readily respond. The Church Missionary Society have had a font of type cast in this new character, and several little tracts have been printed and circulated among the tribe. The principal inventor of this alphabet is now dead; but it is supposed that he died in the Christian faith, having acquired some knowledge of the way of salvation through the medium of this character of his own invention.† Dr. Wilson says :

* Africa and the American Flag," p. 52.
† Wilson's " Western Africa," p. 95, and " Princeton Review for July 1858," p. 488.

This invention is one of the most remarkable achievements of this or any other age, and is itself enough to silence forever the cavils and sneers of those who think so contemptuously of the intellectual endowments of the African race.

Though "the idea of communciating thoughts in writing was probably suggested by the use of Arabic among the Mandingoes," yet the invention was properly original, showing the existence of genius in the native African who has never been in foreign slavery, and proves that he carries in his bosom germs of intellectual development and self-elevation, which would have enabled him to advance regularly in the path of progress had it not been for the blighting influence of the slave-trade.

Now are we to believe that such a people have been doomed, by the terms of any curse, to be the "servant of servants," as some upholders of Negro slavery have taught? Would it not have been a very singular theory that a people destined to servitude should begin, the very first thing, as we have endeavored to show, to found "great cities," organize kingdoms, and establish rule—putting up structures which have come down to this day as a witness to their *superiority* over all their contemporaries—and that, by a Providential decree, the people whom they had been fated to serve should be held in bondage by them four hundred years?

The remarkable enterprise of the Cushite hero, Nimrod; his establishment of imperial power, as an advance on patriarchal government; the strength of the Egypt of Mizraim, and its long domination over the house of Israel; and the evidence which now and then appears, that even Phut (who is the obscurest in his fortunes of all the Hamite race) maintained a relation to the descendants of Shem which was far from servile or subject; do all clearly tend to limit the application of Noah's maledictory prophecy to the precise terms in which it was indited: "Cursed be Canaan; a servant of servants shall he" (not Cush, not Mizraim, not Phut, but he) "be to his brethren." If we then confine the imprecation to Canaan, we can without difficulty trace its accomplishment in the subjugation of the tribes which issued from him to the children of Israel from the time of Joshua to that of David. Here would be verified Canaan's servile relation to Shem; and when imperial Rome finally wrested the scepter from Judah, and, "dwelling in the tents of Shem," occupied the East and whatever remnants of Canaan were left in it, would not this accomplish that further prediction that Japheth, too, should be lord of Canaan, and that (as it would seem to be tacitly implied) mediately, through his occupancy of the tents of Shem ? *

A vigorous writer in the "Princeton Review" has the following:

The Ethiopian race, from whom the modern Negro or African stock are undoubtedly descended, can claim as early a history, with the exception of the Jews,† as any living people on the face of the earth. History, as well as the monumental discoveries, gives them a place in ancient history as far back as Egypt herself, if not farther. But what has become of the contemporaneous nations of antiquity, as well as others of much later origin ? Where are the Numidians, Mauritanians, and other powerful names, who once held sway over all Northern Africa ! They have been swept away from the earth, or dwindled down to a handful of modern Copts and Berbers of doubtful descent.

The Ethiopian, or African race, on the other hand, though they have long since lost all the civilization which once existed on the Upper Nile, have, nevertheless, continued to increase and multiply, until they are now, with the exception of the Chinese, the largest single family of men on the face of the earth. They have extended themselves in every direction over that great continent, from the southern borders of the Great Sahara to the Cape of Good Hope, and from the Atlantic to the Indian Ocean, and are thus constituted masters of at least three fourths of the habitable portions of this great continent. And this progress has been made, be it remembered, in despite of the prevalence of the foreign slave-trade, which has carried off so many of their people; of the ceaseless internal feuds and wars that have been waged among themselves ; and of a conspiracy, as it were, among all surrounding nations, to trample out their national existence. Surely their history is a remarkable one; but not more so, perhaps, than is foreshadowed in the prophecies of the Old Testament Scriptures. God has watched over and preserved these people through all the vicissitudes of their unwritten history, and no doubt for some great purpose of mercy toward them, as well as for the display of the glory of his own grace and providence ; and we may expect to have a full revelation of this purpose and glory as soon as the everlasting Gospel is made known to these benighted millions.‡

One palpable reason may be assigned why the Ethiopian race has continued to exist under the most adverse circumstances, while other races and tribes have perished from the earth; it is this: *they have never been a blood-thirsty or avaricious people.* From the beginning of their history to the present time their work has been constructive, except when they have

---

* Dr. Peter Holmes, Oxford, England.
† The Jews not excepted. Where were they when the Pyramids were built ?
‡ "Princeton Review, July 1858," pp. 448, 449.

been stimulated to wasting wars by the covetous foreigner. They have *built up* in Asia, Africa, and America. They have not delighted in despoiling and oppressing others. The nations enumerated by the reviewer just quoted, and others besides them—all warlike and fighting nations—have passed away or dwindled into utter insignificance. They seem to have been consumed by their own fierce internal passions. The Ethiopians, though brave and powerful, were not a fighting people, that is, were not fond of fighting for the sake of humbling and impoverishing other people. Every reader of history will remember the straightforward, brave, and truly Christian answer returned by the King of the Ethiopians to Cambyses, who was contemplating an invasion of Ethiopia, as recorded by Herodotus. For the sake of those who may not have access to that work we reproduce the narrative here. About five hundred years before Christ, Cambyses, the great Persian warrior, while invading Egypt, planned an expedition against the Ethiopians; but before proceeding upon the belligerent enterprises he sent

"Spies in the first instance, who were to see the table of the sun, which was said to exist among the Ethiopians, and besides, to explore other things, and, to cover their design, they were to carry presents to the King. . . . When the messengers of Cambyses arrived among the Ethiopians they gave the presents to the King, and addressed him as follows: "Cambyses, King of the Persians, desirous of becoming your friend and ally, has sent us, bidding us confer with you, and he presents you with these gifts, which are such as he himself most delights in."

But the Ethiopian knowing that they came as spies, spoke thus to them:

"Neither has the King of Persia sent you with these presents to me because he valued my alliance, nor do you speak the truth, for you are come as spies of my kingdom. Nor is he a just man; for if he were just he would not desire any other territory than his own; nor would he reduce people into servitude who have done him no injury. However, give him this bow, and say these words to him: 'The King of the Ethiopians advises the King of the Persians, when the Persians can thus easily draw a bow of this size, then to make war on the Macrobian Ethiopians with more numerous forces; but until that time let him thank the gods, who have not inspired the sons of the Ethiopians with the desire of adding another land to their own.'"*

* Herodotus, iii, 17–22.

24

Are these a people, with such remarkable antecedents, and in the whole of whose history the hand of God is so plainly seen, to be treated with the contempt which they usually suffer in the lands of their bondage? When we notice the scornful indifference with which the Negro is spoken of by certain politicians in America, we fancy that the attitude of Pharaoh and the aristocratic Egyptians must have been precisely similar toward the Jews. We fancy we see one of the magicians in council, after the first visit of Moses demanding the release of the Israelites, rising up with indignation and pouring out a torrent of scornful invective such as any rabid anti-Negro politician might now indulge in.

What privileges are those that these degraded Hebrews are craving? What are they? Are they not slaves and the descendants of slaves? What have they or their ancestors ever done? What *can* they do? They did not come hither of their own accord. The first of them was brought to this country a slave, sold to us by his own brethren. Others followed him, refugees from the famine of an impoverished country. What do they know about managing liberty or controlling themselves? They are idle; they are idle. Divert their attention from their idle dreams by additional labor and more exacting tasks.

But what have the ancestors of Negroes ever done? Let Professor Rawlinson answer, as a summing up of our discussion. Says the learned Professor:

For the last three thousand years the world has been mainly indebted for its advancement to the Semitic and Indo-European races; *but it was otherwise in the first ages.* Egypt and Babylon, Mizraim and Nimrod—both descendants of Ham— led the way, and acted as the pioneers of mankind in the various untrodden fields of art, literature, and science. Alphabetic writing, astronomy, history, chronology, architecture, plastic art, sculpture, navigation, agriculture, textile industry, seem all of them to have had their origin in one or other of these two countries. The beginnings may have been often humble enough. We may laugh at the rude picture-writing, the uncouth brick pyramid, the coarse fabric, the homely and ill-shapen instruments, as they present themselves to our notice in the remains of these ancient nations; but they are really worthier of our admiration than of our ridicule. The inventors of any art are among the greatest benefactors of their race, and mankind at the present day lies under infinite obligations to the genius of these early ages.*

* "Five Great Monarchies," vol. i, pp. 75, 76.

There are now, probably, few thoughtful and cultivated men in the United States who are prepared to advocate the application of the curse of Noah to all the descendants of Ham. The experience of the last eight years must have convinced the most ardent theorizer on the subject. Facts have not borne out their theory and predictions concerning the race. The Lord by his outstretched arm has dashed their syllogisms to atoms, scattered their dogmas to the winds, detected the partiality and exaggerating tendency of their method, and shown the injustice of that heartless philosophy and that unrelenting theology which consigned a whole race of men to hopeless and interminable servitude.

It is difficult, nevertheless, to understand how, with the history of the past accessible, the facts of the present before their eyes, and the prospect of a clouded future, or unvailed only to disclose the indefinite numerical increase of Europians in the land, the blacks of the United States can hope for any distinct, appreciable influence in the country. We cannot perceive on what grounds the most sanguine among their friends can suppose that there will be so decisive a revolution of popular feeling in favor of their *protegés* as to make them at once the political and social equals of their former masters. Legislation cannot secure them this equality in the United States any more than it has secured it for the blacks in the West Indies. During the time of slavery every thing in the laws, in the customs, in the education of the people was contrived with the single view of degrading the Negro in his own estimafion and that of others. Now is it possible to change in a day the habits and character which centuries of oppression have entailed? We think not. More than one generation, it appears to us, must pass away before the full effect of education, enlightenment, and social improvement will be visible among the blacks. Meanwhile they are being gradually absorbed by the Caucasian; and before their social equality comes to be conceded they will have lost their identity altogether, a result, in our opinion, extremely undesirable, as we believe that, as Negroes, they might accomplish a great work which others cannot perform. But even if they should not pass away in the mighty embrace of their numerous white neighbors; grant that they could continue to live in the land, a distinct people, with the marked peculiarities they possess, having the same color and hair, badges of a former thraldom —is it to be supposed that they can ever overtake a people who so largely outnumber them, and a large proportion of whom are endowed with wealth, leisure, and the habits and means of study and self-improvement? If they improve in culture and training, as in time they no doubt will, and become intelligent and educated, there may rise up individuals among them, here and there, who will be respected and honored by the whites; but it is plain that, as a class, their inferiority will never cease until they cease to be a distinct people, possessing peculiarities which suggest antecedents of servility and degradation.

We pen these lines with the most solemn feelings—grieved that so many strong, intelligent, and energetic black men should be wasting time and labor in a fruitless contest, which, expended in the primitive land of their fathers—a land that so much needs them—would produce in a comparatively short time results of incalculable importance. But what can we do? Occupying this distant stand-point—an area of Negro freedom and a scene for untrammeled growth and development, but a wide and ever-expanding field for benevolent effort; an outlying or surrounding wilderness to be reclaimed; barbarism of ages to be brought over to Christian life—we can only repeat with undiminished earnestness the wish we have frequently expressed elsewhere, that the *eyes of the blacks may be opened to discern their true mission and destiny;* that, making their escape from the house of bondage, they may *betake themselves to their ancestral home, and assist in constructing a Christian* AFRICAN EMPIRE. For we believe that as descendants of Ham had a share, as the most prominent actors on the scene, in the founding of cities and in the organization of government, so members of the same family, developed under different circumstances, will have an important part in the closing of the great drama.

"Time's noblest offspring is the last."